KU-720-298

OPAL DUNN is a well-known specialist in early first and second language development. She has been a consultant to the Council of Europe on children's bilingual education. In 2008, she received the Japanese Order of the Rising Sun for over 30 years' work with Japanese children. She has written numerous children's books for Frances Lincoln.

PATRICE AGGS was born in Detroit, Michigan and studied at St Johns College, Annapolis and at the City & Guilds Art School in London. Patrice has illustrated more than 50 children's books, including *Uno Dos Tres* for Frances Lincoln, and has produced etchings and watercolours now in collections in Europe, the US and Japan.

The compiler and the publisher believe that all the material in this collection is traditional and in the public domain. If any errors or omissions have occured, the publisher will be pleased to rectify these at the earliest opportunity.

Text copyright © Opal Dunn 1995
Illustrations copyright © Patrice Aggs 1995

The right of Opal Dunn to be identified as the author and of Patrice Aggs to be identified as the illustrator of this work has been asserted by them in accordance with the Copyright, Designs and Patents Act, 1988 (United Kingdom).

First published in Great Britain in 1996 and in the USA in 1996 by Frances Lincoln Children's Books, 74-77 White Lion Street, London N1 9PF www.franceslincoln.com

This edition published in 2006

All rights reserved

No part of this publication may be reproduced, stored in a retrieval system, or transmitted, in any form, or by any means, electrical, mechanical, photocopying, recording or otherwise without the prior written permission of the publisher or a licence permitting restricted copying. In the United Kingdom such licences are issued by the Copyright Licensing Agency, Saffron House, 6-10 Kirby Street, London EC1N 8TS.

A catalogue record for this book is available from the British Library

ISBN 978-1-84507-623-8

Printed in China

9

Deux Trois

FIRST FRENCH RHYMES

Selected by
OPAL DUNN

Illustrated by
PATRICE AGGS

F

FRANCES LINCOLN
CHILDREN'S BOOKS

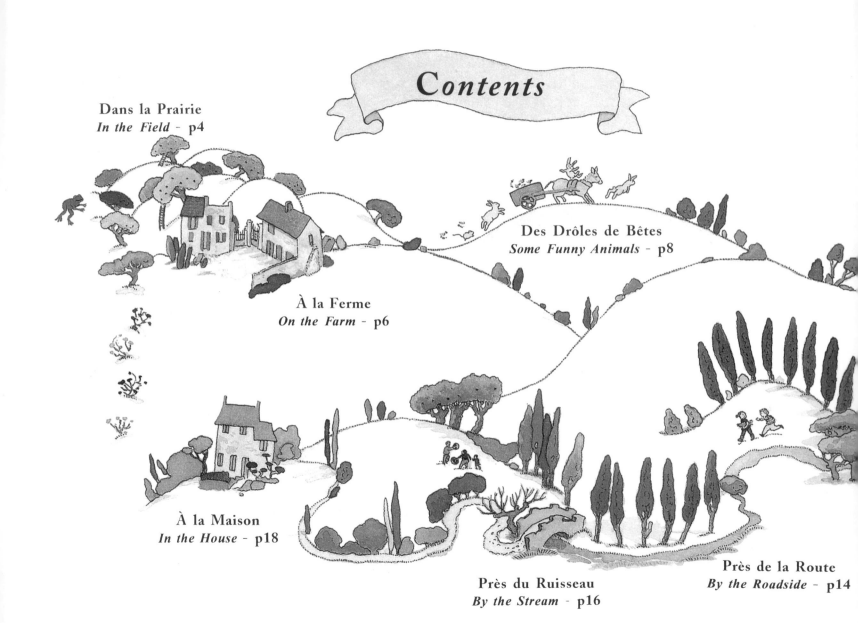

Contents

Un Deux Trois

Autour du Marché
Around the Market - p10

Au Café
At the Café - p12

From the many traditional rhymes known to generations
of French-speaking children, I have selected these few as
an enjoyable and useful introduction to learning French.
Each rhyme has special qualities for helping with difficult sounds
or using difficult language; some are games, others are songs.
In the same way as children pick up rhymes in their
own language, they will easily pick up rhymes in French.
If they listen to the lively recording made by French children
(which accompanies the book), they are sure to absorb correct
intonation and pronounciation. Praise and encouragement
from you helps to make learning more successful!

I have arranged the rhymes to take you on a journey,
which you can follow in the *Contents* picture on the left.
Colourful illustrations depict each scene, from the fields to
the market place, and help the child work out the meaning
of the language. On every page, key words are illustrated
and labelled. The *Guide* at the back of the book explains
the rhymes and how some are played. Useful phrases are
highlighted for children to use in simple conversations.

Join me on a journey
and see how learning French can be fun!

Opal Dunn

Une pomme verte,
Une pomme rouge,
Une pomme d'or,
C'est toi qui es dehors.

une pomme d'or

Am stram gram
Pic et pic et colégram
Bourre et bourre et ratatam
Am stram gram.

une grenouille

une échelle

Dans la Prairie

une pomme rouge

Une grenouille nouille nouille,
Qui se croyait belle belle belle,
Montait à l'échelle chelle chelle,
Et redescendait dait dait,
Et se cassant le nez nez nez.
C'est à toi de chercher.

En été   En automne

Au printemps

En hiver

un petit chemin

une poule

du pain

À *la* Ferme

Au printemps, je te réjouis,

En été, je te rafraîchis.

En automne, je te nourris bien,

En hiver, je te chauffe pour rien.

Devinez qui je suis . . .
Un pommier.

Plote!

Dans la cour de chez Dubois

Il y a sept oies:

Une oie, deux oies, trois oies,

Quatre oies, cinq oies, six oies,

C'est toi!

Une poule sur un mur

Qui picote du pain dur,

Picoti, picota,

Lève la queue

Et puis s'en va

Par ce petit chemin là.

une oie

une queue

7
sept

le châlet

PARIS

Des Drôles de Bêtes

Le petit rat, rat, rat,
Du châlet, let, let,
À Paris, ris, ris,
Est allé, lé, lé,
Sur le dos, dos, dos,
D'un mulet, let, let,
N'a trouvé, vé, vé,
Pour manger, ger, ger,
Qu'un radis pourri.

un gros rat

un petit rat

Aa, Bb, Cc,
J'ai gagné,
Oo, Pp, Qq,
J'ai perdu
Mon petit cheval
De cent écus.

un mulet

un cheval

Le lapin,
    Qui a du chagrin.
La fourmi,
    Qui a du souci.
Et le petit rat,
    Qui a du tracas.
Oh là là!
    Comment arranger tout ça?

un radis

un lapin

une fourmi

Mes oeufs,

Mes beaux oeufs sont frais,

Pas vrai?

Et voilà les petits,

Et voilà les gros,

Et voilà les petits patés tout chauds.

un oeuf

une poule

une pêche

un gros paté

un petit paté

Autour du Marché

un chapeau

C'est la dame aux petits carreaux
Qui vend des chapeaux,
Rue des Petits Manteaux,
Numéro zéro.

un chapeau
dans une boite

Pêche, pomme, poire, abricot,
Y'en a une, y'en a une.
Pêche, pomme, poire, abricot,
Y'en a une de trop.
Qui s'appelle Marie Margot?

une poire

un abricot

une pomme

Au Café

Qui fait un?

    Moi tout seul.

Qui fait deux?

    Les oreilles du vieux.

Qui fait trois?

    Les yeux et le nez.

Qui fait quatre?

    Les genoux et les coudes.

Qui fait cinq?

    Les doigts de ma main.

Qui fait six?

    Les narines, les jambes, les bras.

Qui fait sept?

    Les trous dans la tête.

Bonjour Madame Lundi,
Comment va Madame Mardi?
Très bien Madame Mercredi:
Dites à Madame Jeudi
De venir Vendredi
Car je pars Samedi
Pour arriver Dimanche.

les narines
la main
les yeux
une rose
la bouche
les cheveux
les doigts

J'ai une rose
Dans les cheveux.
Prends-la, si tu veux.

Beau front,
Beaux yeux,
Nez de cancan,
Bouche d'argent
Menton fleuri
Guili-guili-guili.

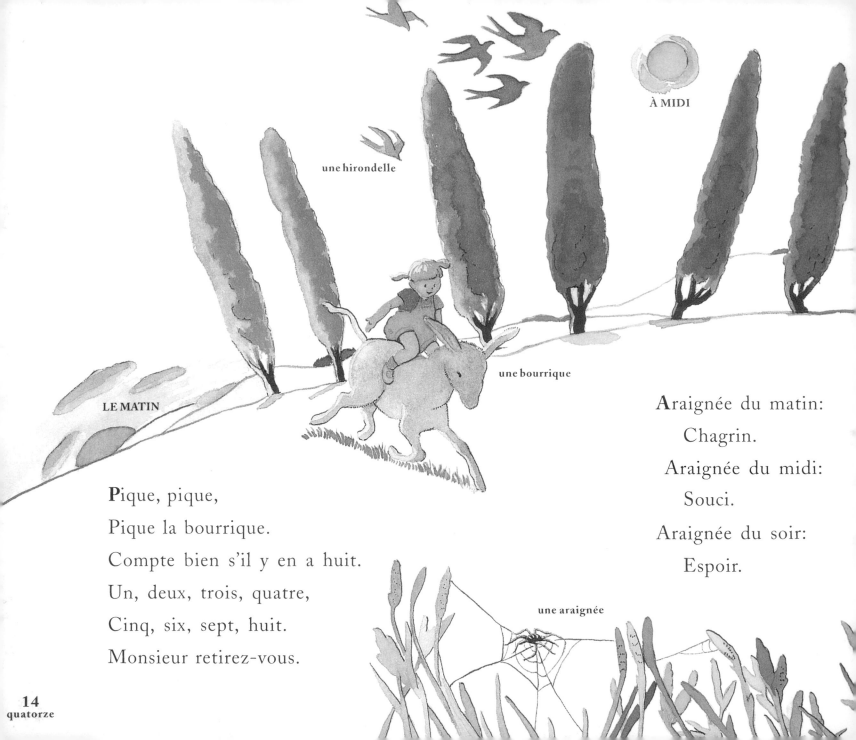

une hirondelle

À MIDI

LE MATIN

une bourrique

Araignée du matin:

Chagrin.

Araignée du midi:

Souci.

Araignée du soir:

Espoir.

Pique, pique,

Pique la bourrique.

Compte bien s'il y en a huit.

Un, deux, trois, quatre,

Cinq, six, sept, huit.

Monsieur retirez-vous.

une araignée

Près de la Route

LE SOIR

Cinq hirondelles,
Dix hirondelles,
Quinze hirondelles,
Qu'attendent-elles?
D'autres hirondelles?
Combien seront-elles?
Des dizaines,
Et des dizaines d'hirondelles.
Où iront-elles?

Près du Ruisseau

une perdrix

Do, ré, mi,
La perdrix.
Mi, fa, sol,
Elle s'en vole.
Fa, mi, ré,
Dans un pré.
Mi, ré, do,
Tombe dans l'eau.

Petit poisson qui tourne en rond,
Petit poisson dis-moi ton nom.
Petit poisson qui bouge,
Petit poisson tout rouge,
Petit poisson dis-moi ton nom.

un petit
poisson

Un, deux, trois,

Je m'en vais au bois.

Quatre, cinq, six,

Cueillir des cerises.

Sept, huit, neuf,

Dans mon panier neuf.

Dix, onze, douze,

Elles seront toutes rouges.

un panier

un paysan

une cerise

une grenouille

un grand poisson

Il pleut, il mouille:

C'est la fête à la grenouille.

Il fait beau temps:

C'est la fête au paysan.

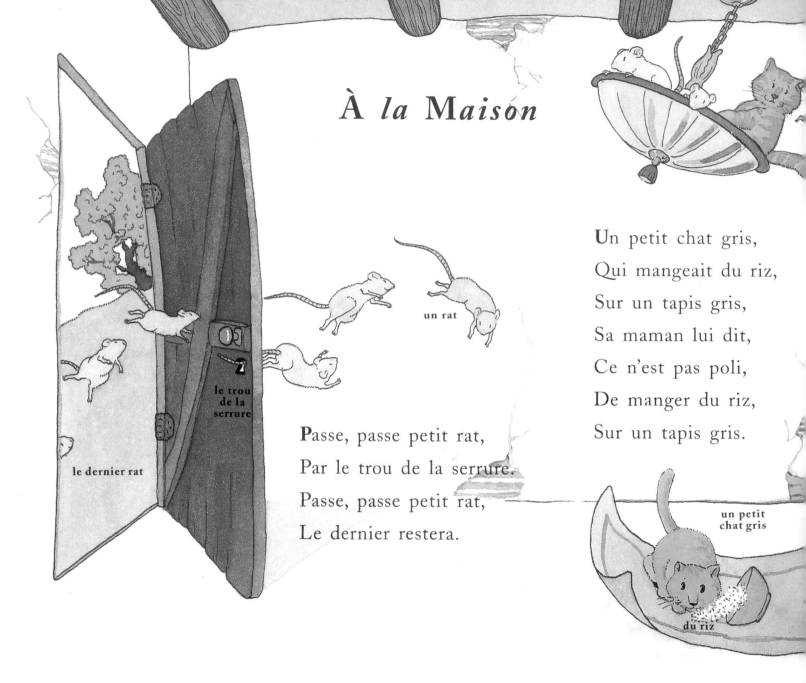

À *la Maison*

un rat

le trou
de la
serrure

le dernier rat

Passe, passe petit rat,
Par le trou de la serrure.
Passe, passe petit rat,
Le dernier restera.

Un petit chat gris,
Qui mangeait du riz,
Sur un tapis gris,
Sa maman lui dit,
Ce n'est pas poli,
De manger du riz,
Sur un tapis gris.

un petit
chat gris

du riz

une souris

Dansons la capucine
Y'a pas de pain chez nous,
Y'en a chez la voisine
Mais ce n'est pas pour nous,
Youp!

une capucine

du pain

un mur

Jamais on n'a vu, vu, vu,
Jamais on ne verra, ra, ra,
Un nid de souris, ris, ris,
Dans l'oreille d'un chat, chat, chat.

Mur usé,
Trou s'y fit,
Rat s'y mit,
Chat l'y prit.

un chat

un trou

un tapis gris

Dans la Prairie - *In the Field* p4

Useful phrases: **c'est toi** - *it's you*
c'est à toi - *it's your turn*

Une Pomme Verte - *One Green Apple*
A 'starting' game used for selecting a leader or 'catcher'. One child stands in the middle of a circle and taps each child in turn as they say the rhyme together. The child on whom the final syllable of the word **'dehors'** (*out*) falls, is eliminated. The game starts again and continues until only one child is left.

Am Stram Gram
A starting game played as **Une Pomme Verte**, counting twenty syllables. All the words are nonsense words, similar to the words in the English rhyme 'Eeny Meeny Miny Mo'.

Une Grenouille - *A Frog*
A starting game to decide which child will be the catcher. Played as **Une Pomme Verte**, but saying the rhyme only once, as the final line of the rhyme **'C'est à toi de chercher'** (*It's your turn to look*), decides who is the catcher. The rhyme is about a frog who thought he was beautiful. He climbed up a ladder and on his way down, he broke his nose!

À la Ferme - *On the Farm* p6

Useful phrases: **pour rien** - *for nothing*
s'en va - *go away*
il y a - *there is*

Au Printemps - *In Spring*
A riddle to help learn the names of the seasons.
In Spring I make you happy / In Summer I refresh you / In Autumn I feed you well / In Winter I keep you warm for nothing / What am I? . . . An apple tree.

Dans la Cour - *In the Yard*
A starting game played as **Une Grenouille**, generally used to find the catcher or leader of a game, **'C'est toi!'** (*It's you!*)

Une Poule - *A Hen*
Played as **Une Pomme Verte**. The child on whom the final syllable of the rhyme **'là'** (*there*) falls, is 'out'. The game ends when there is only one child left.

Des Drôles de Bêtes - *Some Funny Animals* p8

Useful phrases: **comment arranger tout ça?** - *How can we fix all that?*
j'ai gagné - *I've won*
j'ai perdu - *I've lost*

Le Petit Rat - *The Little Rat*
A fun rhyme introducing the different ways of pronouncing the letter 'r' in the French language. The rhyme is about a little rat from the country house who went to Paris on the back of a mule. In Paris he found nothing to eat but **'un radis pourri'** (*a rotten radish*)!

Comment Arranger Tout Ça? - *How Can We Fix All That?*
A rhyme playing with sounds and stimulating thoughts about feelings.
The rabbit who is sad / The ant who is worried / And the little rat who has some troubles / Oh dear, dear / How can we fix all that?

Aa Bb Cc
A fun rhyme playing with alphabet letters and giving useful practice with the difficult sound found in **'Qq'**, **'perdu'**, **'écus'**.

Autour du Marché - *Around the Market* p10

Useful phrases: **pas vrai?** - *isn't it true?*
y'en a une - *there's one*
y'en a une de trop - *there's one too many*
voilà - *there is/are*

Mes Oeufs and Les Petits Patés - *My Eggs and the Small Patés*
These are typical cries that can be heard in street markets in French-speaking countries. They are useful in exploring how to use adjectives:
My beautiful eggs are fresh / And there are little / And there are big / And there are little pates all nice and hot.

Rue des Petits Manteaux, Numéro Zéro - *Little Coat Street, Number Zero*
A fun rhyme playing with consonants about a lady who sells hats from a shop in **'Rue des Petits Manteaux'**.

Pêche, Pomme, Poire, Abricot - *Peach, Apple, Pear, Apricot*
Played as **Une Pomme Verte**, eliminating the child on whom the last syllable of the rhyme falls. The rhyme is repeated until only one child remains. This rhyme helps children to absorb different ways of using language, eg., **'Y'en a une de trop'** (*there's one too many*).

u Café - *At the Cafe* p12

seful phrases: **qui fait six?** - *what makes six?*
comment va Madame Mardi? - *how is Mrs Tuesday?*
très bien - *very good*
dites à Madame - *tell madam*
je pars samedi - *I'm leaving on Saturday*
prends-la - *take it*
si tu veux - *if you want*
nez de cancan - *snub nose*

Moi Tout Seul - *Me By Myself*
A counting rhyme which introduces names of the parts of the body.
It can be used as an action rhyme, with the child touching the various parts of
his/her body, including a different way of looking at the head '**Qui fait sept?/
Les trous dans la tête**' (*What makes seven? / The holes in the head*).

Bonjour Madame Lundi - *Good Morning Mrs Monday*
A rhyme to learn the days of the week.

J'ai une Rose - *I Have a Rose*
A simple rhyme: *I have a rose / In my hair / Take it / If you want.*

Beau Front, Beaux Yeux - *Beautiful Forehead, Beautiful Eyes*
An action rhyme for the very young which ends in '**Guili-guili-guili**'
(words without meaning), as the parent tickles the child under his/her chin.

Près de la Route - *By the Roadside* p14

Useful phrases: **compte bien** - *count carefully*
qu'attendent-elles? - *what are they waiting for?*
d'autres - *some other/others*
des dizaines et des dizaines - *dozens and dozens*

La Bourrique - *The Donkey*
Played as **Une Pomme Verte**. Change Monsieur in the last line
to Mademoiselle to fit the sex of the children playing the game.

Araignée du Matin - *Spider in the Morning*
A country saying uttered when seeing a spider or spider's web.
Useful rhyme for learning the different times of the day.
*A spider in the morning / Sorrow / A spider at midday / Worry /
A spider in the evening / Hope.*

Les Hirondelles - *The Swallows*
A rhyme counting swallows which ends by asking '**Où iront-elles?**'
(*Where will they go to?*)

Près du Ruisseau - *By the Stream* p16

Useful phrases: **dis-moi ton nom** - *tell me your name*
c'est la fête - *it's the celebration*
elle s'en vole - *she flies away*
il fait beau temps - *it's good weather*

Petit Poisson - *Little Fish*
A simple rhyme with useful phrases. *Little fish turning in a circle /
Little fish tell me your name / Little fish moving /
Little fish who is red all over / Little fish tell me your name.*

Do Ré Mi, La Perdrix - *Doh Ray Me, The Partridge*
A song using the musical scale.

Un, Deux, Trois, Je m'en Vais au Bois - *One, Two, Three, I'm Off to the Woods*
A counting song about going to the woods
To collect cherries / In my new basket / They'll all be red.

Il Pleut, Il Mouille - *It's Raining, It's Soaking*
A country saying about the weather. *It's raining, it's soaking / It's celebration
time for frogs / It's good weather / It's celebration time for farmers.*

À la Maison - *In the House* p18

Useful phrases: **ce n'est pas poli** - *it's not polite*
y'a pas - *there isn't any*
chez nous - *at our house*
chez la voisine - *at the neighbours*
ce n'est pas pour nous - *that's not for us*

Passe, Passe Petit Rat - *Pass, Pass Little Rat*
Similar to '*Oranges and Lemons*' when two children join hands to make
an arch. On the last syllable of '**restera**' (*stays behind*), the two children
drop their arms to trap the child who's under the arch.

Un Petit Chat Gris - *A Little Grey Cat*
An amusing, repetitive rhyme. *A little grey cat / Who ate some rice / On a grey
carpet / His mother told him / It's not polite / To eat rice / On a grey carpet.*

Jamais on n'a Vu, Jamais on ne Verra - *Never Has Anyone Seen,
Never Will Anyone See*
A song repeating sounds that are difficult to pronounce like '**vu**', '**ra**', '**riz**'.
Never has anyone seen / Never will anyone see / A mice nest / In a cat's ear.

Dansons la Capucine - *The Nasturtium Dance*
Similar to '*Ring O' Roses*'. This rhyme is full of useful phrases (see above).

Mur Usé - *Old Wall*
This short rhyme tells a whole story in four compact phrases.
It tells the story of an *Old wall / In which a hole is made /
A rat goes into the hole / The cat catches the rat in the hole.*